For Fay Hillier. E.D.
For Eoin. H.R.

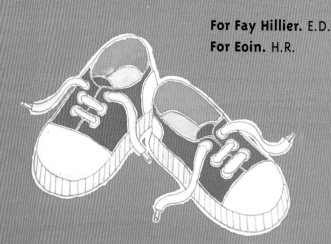

Copyright © 1999 Zero to Ten Limited
Illustrations copyright © 1999 Emma Dodd
Text copyright © 1999 Hannah Reidy

Publisher: Anna McQuinn • Art Director: Tim Foster
First published in the United States in 1999
by Zero To Ten Ltd, 95 Madison Avenue, New York, NY 10016
and distributed by Larousse Kingfisher Chambers

ISBN 1-84089-152-1

Printed in Mexico.

Library of Congress Cataloging-in-Publication Data

Reidy, Hannah.
What do you like to wear? / written by Hannah Reidy,
illustrated by Emma Dodd
    p. cm. - - (In between books)

Summary: Examines various articles of clothing worn fo
different occasions, while introducing descriptive word
such as "furry," "itchy," and "frilly."
    ISBN 1-84089-152-1
1. Children's clothing--Juvenile literature. [1.Clothing a
dress.] I. Dodd, Emma 1969- ill. II. Title. III. Series:
Reidy, Hannah. In between books.

TT635.R45 1999
646.4'06--dc21
                                                98-447

What do you like to wear?

Written by Hannah Reidy
Illustrated by Emma Dodd

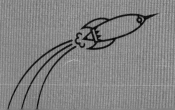

Becky loves her **checked** shirt, she wears it when she's working.

Cody's **furry** collar keeps him **nice** and **warm.**

Owen loves his
buzzy bee suit.

Oscar prefers his **BIG BOY** clothes.

Isaac doesn't like his **itchy** sweater.

He'd rather wear his **soft** sweatshirt.

Louise wears her **frilly** dress for parties.

Louie wears his **frilly** shirt.

Liam's baseball cap looks **cool** with his Dad's new **sunglasses.**

Pippa has lots of **pockets** all over her **striped** overalls.

Toby's **teddy** pajamas are **soft** and **warm** and perfect for dreaming.

What do you